Waves Of Enchantment

Waves crash and foam at the
tips of crystal sand
As the wind sends ripples to
shimmer the tide
Sending whispers to echo in the
distant surf
I hear your laughter, melodious
as a gentle song
Cascading across a summer
breeze
Your face bright and clear as
the sun
Glistening on a carpet of blue-
green sea
My heart pulls on its string at
the sound of your voice
As we walk along a starlit shore
Content in sweet surrender
But lays still with but a simple
beat
Left enchanted, and nothing
more

Dancing for Tomorrow

Tonight's the night
We're going to dance away
Today's the day
It's going to go our way

No ones going to tell us
What to do or
What to say
Cause it's going to go our way

Tomorrow will be
The day we are finally free
So we can go out on our own
Without a worry stone

It's the last dance
Our only chance
For true romance

The sun goes down
And we begin to frown
Because the sound
Is winding down

Shining through A look

When you look at me
I can tell what you are thinking
When you look at me
I can tell how you are feeling

When you are happy
Your eyes show it
When you are sad
Your face shows it

No matter what
I can always tell your mood
You try and hide it on the
outside
But I always look deep into
your eyes
To see exactly what kind of
mood you're in

When you're in a good mood
Your voice shows it
When you're in a bad mood
You're not that talkative

So no matter what you do
I can always tell
What kind of mood you're in

Lonely

Sitting,
Alone in the dark
Feeling unloved

Sitting,
Wondering…
If there is anyone for me

Feeling,
Nothing…
But heart ache

Looking,
But not seeing…
Anything except tears
Hitting the ground

Watching,
People together having fun
And me having no fun at all
That is my loneliness

A special note

When I hear a certain tune
It makes me smile
And want to sing

When I hear another tune
It makes me sad
And want to cry

Music plays all the time
Even when we aren't aware of
it
Music is everywhere

In our heads
In our voice
In our ears

But most of all
It's in our life
From day one till the end

Music is apart of us all
That's what makes life so
special

We hear a tune and we get a
certain feeling
Whether it be good or bad

Some music helps us get
through life
Some music helps us end life
But most of all it's apart of
every ones life

Skip of a heartbeat

My heart is beating
Day in and day out,
It never stops

When you come close to me
My heart beats fast
When you talk to me
My heart starts racing

I can never get
You out of my mind,
From the first time I saw you
To the first time I talked to you

I've tried everything I know
To show you how much I care
about you
But it just isn't working
I don't know what else to do
I just want to be with you

You are what I dream of at
night
And what I think about all the

time
I hope one day, one time I get
the chance
To show you romance

You are the only one I want
And nobody else
You are the best
And in my heart you'll never be
a guest

My internal love for you

When you said the words
That broke my heart
I felt my dreams
And world coming to an end

But you are the greatest
Person in my life
I will always keep you in my
heart,
And hope you will do the same

You are the first person
I have ever loved
And I will never forget you
I hope you will never forget me

If asked on my judgment day
You were the first person
I have ever loved and
You have filled most of the
room in my heart

I will always have feelings for
you,

Including life after death
You will always be with me
And nothing can change that

My feelings for you

Night after night
I hear your voice
So lovely and calm

Night after night
I see you smile
So bright and gorgeous in every
way

When you talk
I understand what you mean
And I see the passion burning
in your eyes

Everyone has a wish
Most of them come true
My only wish is to be with you

What you mean to me

When I saw you for the first
time
It felt like nothing I've ever felt
before,
It was love at first sight

Now I am still feeling the same
way
And I want to be with you
But I understand you don't
want a relationship,
You only want to be friends

But no matter what I want you
to see
I will always keep you in my
heart,
And will always remember you

You have been there for me
Through rough times,
Through good times,
And whenever I needed
someone

You mean the world to me
And you always will
I will never forget you as long
as I live

Destruction of lava

Darker and darker
It gets at night
Nothing is a pretty sight

Volcanoes erupt
Streets on fire
There is lava everywhere

People try to stop it
They burn alive
There is still lava everywhere

The whole city is on fire
No one can stop it
Soon all that is left is ash

The ground erupts
And lava comes up
Faster and faster it moves

Taking out other cities
Soon the world will be gone
And people will be no longer

The hurtful day

When you told me
You only wanted to be friends
It hurt me to an extent
Of depression and heart ache

When my friend told me
You weren't interested in me
And I didn't have anything to
offer
I was crushed

I was hurt to hear it all
From a friend instead of you
I really thought we had
something
But I was wrong

I spent all my time on you
Hoping we could have a night
of total bliss
But now I understand
I never had a chance

I hope we can be friends,

And you will always have
A special place in my heart
forever
I will never forget you as long
as I live

When

When you talk to me
It sounds like birds singing in a
tree
When you look at me
All I see is stars in your eyes

When you're next to me
I get chills down my spine,
My heart beats fast
And I get goose bumps on my
arms

When I see you
It's like seeing an angel from
heaven
I just wish time would freeze
So we can be together forever

When I sleep
I dream of you
When I am awake
I just want to be with you

When I am not with you

I feel lonely
When I am with you
I will make everything perfect
For you and me

You Are…

You are as bright as the sun
Your eyes are as beautiful as
the sky
You are like the sun in most
ways
You rise in the morning
And set at night

I compare you to a jogger
Because you are always
running through my head
Without you my life is
incomplete
With you by my side
I have nothing left to fulfill
But to keep you happy forever

If I can't have you
Then there is nothing to live for
If I have you
I will be happy for life

I will remember you
When times are tough

I will remember you
When I am down
But most of all
I will remember you when
you're gone

The road of life

When you said the words
That hurt me
I wished my life away

People say they don't want to
lose me
They care too much about me
I don't know whether I should
believe them
Or if they're make believin

Times are confusing
Things are hard
I just want it to be
Back the way used to be the
two of us you and me

People say wishes come true
But mine never do
So I hate making wishes
I want it simple again

Each day life gets harder
I've been told it gets much

worse
It's a lie it can't be true
A life without you

Crying

I cry at night,
Wondering if...
There is really anyone,
Out there for me

Sometimes I think,
I have found the right person
But then I end up being
wrong,
And get hurt

But I still...
Cry at night
Wondering why,
I was put on this planet

People try to help me,
But then only make things
worse
The only one who can help
me,
Is me because I know what is
wrong

Other people try to
Make me smile
But hey if I wanted to smile
I would so stop trying

That's why I sit alone in my
room
To get away from people,
And think about things,
And cry about the stuff that
hurts

When I think at night,
I wonder if I could ever
Make my dreams come true

The dreams of singing and
touring,
The dreams of finding that
one
Special girl for me,
Whether she is famous or not
I wouldn't care

Those are the main
Reasons that

I sit at night in my room
And just think and let the
Tears hit the ground

Blonde Bombshell

When I first saw
That smooth, long blonde
hair,
And those ocean like blue
eyes

I thought I had
Just seen an angel

You looked so beautiful
And sweet in every way

But then one day
You did something
That was totally unexpected

I gave you my
Heart and thought
You would cherish it,
But the only thing you did
Was break it into a million
pieces

Then you left me
And ran to Florida
You didn't even tell me
Until you got there

I see now
The only thing
You liked to do
Was play with my emotions
And break my heart

And now I still
Think about you
And wonder where I went
wrong

I will remember next time
To never trust anyone
Because of what you did to
me
Mentally and emotionally.

Why did you leave

You said you would never
leave
That we would be together
forever
You left and you lied
Now I am here all alone

No one to talk to
No one to hang out with
No one to listen to
And especially…
No one around who knows
My deepest darkest secrets

You lied to me
And broke our bond
You broke the trust
But most of all
You broke my heart

I am lost without you
I don't know which way is up
Or which way is down

You showed me a good
direction
You told me stay on this path
You told me nothing would go
wrong
Just as everything was going
good
You took off and everything
started going wrong

I have no idea where you are
Or who you are with
Or if you are even ok
All I know is that
You broke the bond of
friendship

Blood of my blood

Blood of my blood
Bone of my bone
There I sat all alone
No one around
Not even a sound

Suddenly I hear something
I look to the left and to the right
But nothing is there
The sound is getting closer

I feel something grab my leg
And pull me down into a grave
And it said to me
"Blood of my blood,
Bone of my bone,
Now I am not alone"

Ocean Experience

It was a warm summers day
In the middle of May
I went to the ocean
To enjoy the waves motion

I walked to the tip of the water
As the day grew hotter
The sand caressed my feet
As I was cooling down from
the heat

As I lie there in the sand
I listen to the live band
Play the soft tune
It was almost noon

I grabbed my board
And put my foot in the cord
I road the wave
Until it turned into a cave

As the waves pushed into my
back
I heard a noise that sounded

like a crack
As I plummeted to the bottom
of the ocean
I could hear the loud
commotion

I looked down at my legs
And they just looked like pegs
The wind was knocked out of
me
I tried to look around but I
couldn't see

I floated to the top
And I suddenly felt a pop
I went to feel my knee
But I remembered I couldn't
see

The doctor said I was paralyzed
from the waist down
Hearing this news made me
frown
I will never forget that warm
summers day
In the middle of May

Dark Hours

Dark hours, by which once
more I stand
Alone in the cemetery
Bodies everywhere
Caskets still not buried
Gruesome bodies
In which I see with my own
eyes
I get close to one to touch it,
I want to see what it feels like
As I touch it, its eyes open
And it grabs me by the throat
I now know,
In the dark hours, by which
once more
I stand that I am not alone

Hard Times

When you left me
I felt my life coming to an end
I had no place to go…
I had no one to talk to
I thought death was the way to
go

Day in and day out
I planned my death
After a few weeks
I put my plan into action
On that day I slipped and broke
my leg

So I lived with the pain
In my heart and in my leg
I took medicine to heel the pain
in my leg
But I knew it would never heel
the pain in my heart
You hurt me more than
anything in the world

After a few months of pain

I learned you weren't worth the
pain of death,
I learned love could be
replaced,
I learned a broken leg hurts
But not as much as a broken
heart

On this day,
I say to you,
Go away and leave me alone
You're not worth my time,
And you're not worth another
heartbreak

First Glance

When I first saw you
I got a feeling like none other
When I first looked into your
eyes
I saw beauty like never before

Your long black hair
Reminds me of the night
It feels so soft
When I run my hands through it

I just want one special night
To show you bliss and romance
I want to show you
My true feelings

Just one night
Of fun and excitement
I just want to
Look into your eyes forever

I don't want anymore
And I can handle less
This I have wanted

To tell you for a while

Mystery Girl

You are so mysterious
And it is really hard
To figure you out

I want to get
To know you and
Find out what you're truly
about

I see you everyday
I hear your lovely voice
And see your beautiful eyes

I just want to
Run my hands
Through your short brown hair

I want to look
Deep into your eyes
And find out your true feelings

I just want to
Spend one night
All alone with you

I just want to
Show you how I feel
About you and only you

I want to show you
One true night of romance
Just you and me

I wish I could
Explain my feelings to you
But I don't know
How to really show you

Good Times

It was a dark night
And three drinks later
I had just gotten through a
break up
And went to the bar
Five drinks after that
I was getting buzzed
I decided it was time
For the true fun
I went out rented a plane and
pilot,
I put on my suit
I grabbed my parachute
And got ready to jump
2800 miles in the air now
I could feel the adrenalin rush,
Or was it the alcohol
All I know was I jumped
And glided my body through
the air
I pulled the chord and shot up,
Then I slowly glided to the
ground
When I hit,

I grabbed the bottle and took a
swig
And then I knew it was…
A total adrenalin rush I felt
Then I knew at that moment
It was truly a good time

Slow and Horrible Pain

Why did you do what you did
You think you went easy
But what you don't know,
Is it really hurt

The pounding in my head
The bleeding that wont stop,
The excruitiating pain inside,
And all you can do is say sorry

You said you would never do
this
And two months later…
You did the unexpected
And left me lying there with
nothing

The dripping on the floor
Big drops making puddles,
The jagged sharp edge in my
side
And there it was…

My heart is in my hand

And your heart next to mine,
The bloody knife lies next to
me
With death knocking on the
door,
And then I am gone forever

Life Without You

I thought it was over
I tried to move on
I let my emotions run wild

And still I was depressed
I tried everything to move on
But the doors slammed in my
face

Night after night
I sit in the dark thinking
After weeks of thinking I
realized one thing

I realized my heart and soul
Belongs to a special person
A person who has been with me
for years

A person who knows me,
Who's been there through thick
and thin,
A person who makes me happy

I have finally realized one thing
I realized who that one person
is
That one special person is you

Roads

The road is rocky and long
There is water everywhere
Unexpected twists and turns
There are even U-turns
Trying to go back...and refresh
That which was lost

But sometimes when you go
back
What was lost is gone forever
You are crushed of the lost
memory
Wishing you would of made
that turn
That turn onto a different road
A road that might have been
smooth traveling

Now your rocky road has more
water
And you are going insane
Trying to find that turn and go

back
But you are too late
The turn is gone
You missed the only chance

Now you are on the rocky road
The rough and wet road
The road of life
The road that is bumpy
And wet full of tears
This is the true…road of life

The race of a lifetime

I flip the switch
And hear the loud noise
I feel the vibration under me
As I move up to the line
slowly

I hear the noise of the people
As I start to rev up
I start to focus on the tree
Three yellow and then the
green

I press the pedal to the floor
As I shoot past the line
And fly down the lane at 215

The power and the force
Slams me to the seat
I move my hand quickly
Shifting and steering

It feels like a lifetime of pain
But as I pass my opponent
I know it will be over soon

I pass the line at the end
Knowing victory is mine
I stop at the end
And take off my helmet

I listen to the announcement
The hear my final time
The voice says loud and clear
I have qualified with a time of
8.87

I jump out and wait for the
crew
As they head over jumping
and screaming
I start getting excited
Finally I made it

This is not a dream I say to
myself
This is all real
My dream has come true
And now I am a record
holding dragster

Unbelievable Pain

It burns into the night
The bigger it gets
The more it burns

I feel the heat
As it burns my skin
The pain is tremendous
But I let it go

I let it burn deeper…
Deeper into my skin it goes
Burning my body and frying
my brain

I am on fire
And I don't care
I know the pain will be gone
soon

As it reaches my heart
I feel the burning sensation
grow

I let it go deeper…

I open my mind
And let it all through
It burns right through
And I am overwhelmed with
joy

I now know
In my mind and heart
What passion really feels like

My Last Chance

I had the chance of a lifetime
And it might have been my last
I said no the first time
Now I am in regret

The time has come
Here and now
To tell the world
How I feel

I let you go far away
It was too far to be
Now you are back
But still to far for me

I was lost without you
Day in and day out
I try to find my way
Back to your heart I look

We spend time alone
It feels like a lifetime
Passing by as we sit under the
tree

Just you and me

We sit and talk
About different things
Then we hit sad roads
You move into my arms
Which I use to hold you

Now feeling like an eternity
I have never had these emotions
before
The feeling of comfort and joy

Eternally Disturbed

The sky is falling
And it's early morning
I was left inside a broken life
That I couldn't wish away
All the days collided
One less perfect than the next

The day you slipped away
Was the day I found
My broken heart just wont be
the same
Because you messed me up
And I'm giving up on
everything

Just when I thought I'd reached
the bottom
Your presence still lingered
here
Your face haunts my once
pleasant dreams
And your voice chased away all
the sanity in me
Without a voice, without a

thought, or a soul
I tried to kill the pain
But only brought on crimson
regret and betrayal

My wounds are crying for the
grave
Immobilized by my fear
And my spirit is sleeping
somewhere cold
Frozen inside without your
touch, without your love
Soon to be blinded by tears
Upon my end shall I begin
forsaking all I've fallen for?

I rise to meet the end
On the way down
I'm screaming, praying,
bleeding
Feeling life coming to an end
My mind is burning with
anguish to get back at you

I don't want your hand this
time

I'll save myself
When I'm alone
I feel so much better
And when I'm with you
I don't feel at all
You just want to mend the
broken wing
Which is that of life

It never was and never will be
Because my escape is hiding
out and running for the door
Cause I can't find you
So take me away
And break me away
I'm dying again...

Special Treasure

There was a time when I was
all alone
Waiting for someone I could
call my own
And when I first looked into
your eyes
I know you were the one

You've got a way with words
And I love the way with just
one whisper
You tell me everything

But when your eyes say it
That's when I know it's true
And the way your kisses, they
always convince me
Your feelings run so deep

I know a moment spent with
you
Is a moment I treasure
I could stay awake just to hear
you breathing

I could spend my life in this
sweet surrender

I feel your heart so close to
mine
I'm wondering what you're
dreaming...
Wondering if it's me you're
seeing
Then I kiss your eyes and thank
god we're together

Why did you go?

You were fine when I saw you
It was great for the time
I learned a lot
And got to know you

A few months later
I got the call
The call I didn't want to hear

It was the worst call
I had ever received
I miss you dearly

The call that you were gone
forever
I can't stand not having you
Here anymore

It is tearing me apart
You shared your life with me
You shared a lot with all who
knew you

If I would've known

That was the last time
I was going to see you

I would have made it more
special
I had no idea how bad it was
I still can't believe it's over

I was happy for all that time
Then a few months later
I get that dreaded call
That you left me

I wish I could tell you
One more time
How much I miss you

How much I enjoy
Being around you
How special you were to me

But instead I had to say
Goodbye forever
And not get that last chance to
have fun

I miss you dearly
And wish there was
Some way I could speak to you
again

Until that time
I will just be sad
And go on with what is left of
my life

Sweet Sensation

I watch as your flame sparks
And you get hotter
But once you have reached the
level of no return
You start to melt into my hand
like an ice cube

Slowly the liquid pours down
the edge of your body
Like the lava from a volcano
after eruption
And the aroma you put off into
the air
Relaxes me so quickly I can't
react

My mind shuts down
And I am calmer than before
Just being in your presence
Is enough to make me feel good

The only thing I hate

Is when your flame runs out
And your sweet aroma dies
down
Then and only then I know
your magic has worked

Broken heart

Fixing the broken pieces
Is harder then thought of
It's like mending a broken wing

Takes time to work
And a lot of love
Something not done overnight

The pain is excruciating
Hardly worth all the time
The effort is worse

Everything goes downhill
And keeps going forever
Or so it seems

All you think about
Is the person
Nothing more or less

Life gets harder
To move on
Without them by your side

Feeling life coming to an end
Almost unbearable to live
through

Trusting you know real friends
Will be there for you
All will come out right again

Mischa

From the ring of endless light
To the beaches of the OC
I see you sitting by the shore

Wondering what is next in life
And wondering what is missing
I see you listening to the words
of the waves

Listening for advice on the
missing link
But don't worry soon what is
missing will be found
And when found it will be
ready to enjoy

As I sit here watching you in
my mind
I am also wondering what is
missing
Then you turn around and see
me

When I see your beautiful eyes

I finally realize what is missing
And that is a friend

Someone to talk to
And to hang out with
But I think it will never happen

Then you get up
And come over to me
And introduce yourself

I finally realize what is missing,
That is a friend like you
Who is always there through
good and bad

Then you ask me
What is missing in your life
And my response is search your
heart for the answer

Pain Inside

There was a time when I was
all alone
I wake up in the mornings
And I've never felt like this
before

I just need to know if I can
breath
Cause in this head my thoughts
are deep
Trying to figure out this life

Feels like I'm living in a slow
hell
It's getting dark, to dark to see
That long black cloud is
coming down

And I wonder
Why do you always do this to
me
I feel your blood turning cold

Can you feel it in your soul?

That my heart is broken
And the pain won't go away

I just need to know if I can
breath
Cause in this head my thoughts
are deep
Trying to figure out this life

I was left to cry there
Grinning with a lost stare
Wishing someone would cure
this pain

And I'm giving up on
everything
What more can I say
But so much for my happy
ending

Invisible To You

I feel invisible to you
But are you aware of how you
make me feel
I'm longing for love and the
logical...

I've gotta make a change,
And take a risk
But I don't now what to say

I'm lost in my thoughts
And it kills me now just to see
you
I try my hardest to forget
everything

Just so I can say those special
words
But I fear rejection
And the demons that come with
it

I'm torn into pieces
And broken up deep inside

Just wishing you can mend the
pieces together

I just need to know
If in your soul
You feel the same way about
me
As I do for you?

Life

Where has my life gone
I sit here alone
A drunken mess

Wishing I could feel true love
just once
But something always goes
wrong
And people wonder why I am
always depressed

I tell them because I don't
wanna spend my time
Watching the world go by
That I'd rather die

But something always
motivates me
To stay alive and well
Just wish I could figure it out

Have I forgotten my own
worth?
Or is it the fact that no one will

Just listen to me to know the
truth

I am trying to let it out
But feel lost in my own mind
Wishing I could find a way out

Why

Where am I going?
Why am I here?
Will I ever get back?
These questions I ask
Not because I am confused
But because I can't find
answers

You said you were there for me
But when I needed you
You were no where to be found

Like you vanished into thin air
You are gone forever
But I still ask myself
Will I ever see you again?

But with no luck
I also get no response
With no response
Comes no answers

And I am still lost
And am still lonely

And still confused
All because you left

True Beauty

From the first day we met
To the first time we said hello
I was hooked…

All I saw was beauty in you
And a great minded person
All I knew was you had me at
hello

But now that you're gone
I don't know what to do
You were the best to hang with

Better than the rest
I wish I could tell you the truth
But not sure if it will help any

For the fact is that
I fear rejection
And the demons that come with
it all

You are always on my mind
And I don't know what to do

I get so confused at times

And signals are always getting
mixed
I hate it when I get the wrong
one
Because it screws everything
up

So I am confessing this to you
now
Hoping I can seek the truth
From you

One way or another
I hope we can still be friends
Cause that would totally rock

Just Look Inside

I'm waiting here in the dark
Trying to figure out
Why everything is so confusing

It's the first time I ever felt this
lonely
Cause you weren't there when I
was scared, I was so alone
Left there grinning with a lost
stare

It hurts that I'm so unwanted
Somebody rip my heart out
And leave me here to bleed

You just shut me out
Too bad that you couldn't see
That in this head my thoughts
are deep

I'm waiting here in the dark
Trying to figure out
Why everything is so confusing

Trying to keep my cool
But it hurts that I'm so
unwanted
I'm wishing my life away

Cause you couldn't see
There is more than meets the
eye
Just look inside

Beauty

The words they can't describe
the emotion
And the emotion can't be
described with words
For I am speechless when it
comes to you

I can't describe in words
How much I feel for you
And I can't show enough
emotion

My emotion is deep for you
So deep that the eye can't see
And the heart can't possibly
comply too it all

The words they come to mind
But yet can't seem to reach the
mouth
For in my eyes you are so much
more than beautiful

Your beauty is that of which I

can't compare to anything
For in my eyes
Your beauty is more than
anything living; past or present

Where Are You

As I sit here alone
All I want to do is find
someone
Then I see her all over

She is stuck in my head
Night after night
I think about her

I think to myself
Is she the one I have been
looking for?
I want to get to know her

Then I see her
I see such beauty
And I think, "can this be"

Has someone finally shown me
my way?
Has someone shown me who I
belong to?
Then it all comes together

I find a way to talk to her
I find a way to get to know her
Now I just need her to know

This is why I write this to you
This person I see all the time
Is you Ashley Massaro

Eyes

You ask but yet you don't
speak
Not a word is spoken
And I know the answer to the
question

The question that hasn't even
been asked yet
How do I know
I see it in your eyes

All answers can be seen
through the eyes
Any feelings or thoughts can be
seen deep in the eyes
Because that is the quickest
way to the heart

The question you ask is what is
your passion
The answer you get is what you
see in my eyes
Those who can see into my
heart only see my passion

It is one that is hidden deep
down
And only shared with certain
people
Others just ask and that is the
response they get

If you can see past my eyes and
into my heart
Then you are lucky enough to
be a chosen one
One that I let deep into my life
and see what I really think
about

My passion is not open to the
public
And my eyes can be deceiving
So what you see could be true
or could be false

If you do see something
amazing and extraordinary
Then you are the one to know
my passion

And know my life without me
saying anything

Bright Light

Night after night
I dream of this bright light
I hear this deep voice say to me
Walk into my light child

I finally see a presence
In this bright light
I stare this presence in the eyes
And say to it, "I am not
ready…"

I am not ready to join the dark
side
I am not ready to walk into the
burning pits
I am not ready to walk into the
fiery pits of hell
I will not go just yet

I will call when I am ready to
join
I say my creator isn't ready for
me yet
So stop calling me and saying

he is
I will know when he is ready.

My Goal

I want to drive someday
I tell this to you
Looking for support

But none is given
I guess I have to do it
On my own

Once I achieve my goal
I will show you
How good I really am

I want to get slammed into the
seat
Just to feel the thrill and the
rush
Of going at high speeds

I have always gotten what I
want
Though I have worked hard for
it all
This is one goal I will achieve

Nothing or no one will stop me
This time I am doing this on
my own
I don't care what anyone says

I feel I have the focus and
determination
To achieve this goal
And make a name for myself in
the racing world

It Was You

Where have you been all my
life
I've been searching for you
And to my avail
You have been right in front of
me

You have been trying to make
me see it
But I have missed all the signs
Now that I have found you
I know I am truly happy

I should've listened to you
from the start
I should've followed my heart
Instead I followed my head
And fell many times

I have fallen down the black
hole
Known as depression and sank
deeply
Until the one day I found you

And it was you that pulled me
out

It was you that made me see the
light again
It was you that made me
wonder why I didn't see it
It was you that changed my
whole world
Without me realizing it until
now

I'll Never…

I'll never tell you a lie
I'll never tell you anything bad
I'll always tell how I love you

How much you mean to me
I'll always miss you
When you are gone

I'll never tell you a lie
I'll never tell you anything bad
I'll always tell how I love you

How I adore you
How I care for you

I'll never betray you
I'll never leave you
I'll always stay true

And I'll never tell you a lie
I'll never tell you anything bad
I'll always tell how I love you

Dream Come True

I listen…
But don't hear
I only understand

I understand
The passion and emotion
That seeps through your words

I feel I've known you forever
You were just a poster on my
wall
Now I see you all the time

You were a dream in my head
Now you are a reality in my life

You are my heaven
And you have my heart

I could sleep all the time
But feel I would be wasting
away without you

With every word you speak

You mean more and more to
me

You are living proof
That dreams come true

You are the locket in my life
You hold something very
amazing
A special treasure never
forgotten

You hold the key and
combination
To something so dear to me
In which I refer to as my heart.

Wedding Bliss

From the time of birth
You have faced life's many
challenges,
On your own
Now you have found each other

You are about to form a bond
In which you will come
together
To enjoy life and overcome
Any challenge still to come
together

Take the time
To remember your special
moment
As it only comes once
With that one special person

Enjoy the time,
And the memories
Remember the great times from
before
And the ones still to come

Remember life as it is
And how it will be after your
special day
Cherish it with the ones you
love
And take the time to let it soak
into your memory

I hope you have a great life
together
And enjoy the bond you have
with each other
Great dreams have come and
passed
Best wishes on making many
more together

Understanding You

Why do you cry?
With tears so light and gentle
I feel them caress my cheek
As I hold you close

I don't know what to do
But to just sit and hold you
Hold you until you are ready
Ready to tell me why you are
crying

It bothers me to know
That something has hurt you
So deep inside
That you can't bring it up to tell
me

Whatever it is
I am here to listen
Whenever you are ready to talk
Just say the words and I will
understand

I just want to understand you

And wish I could feel the pain
that you do
Just look inside to open up
And when you do, you will
realize I am here

How To Say

These words I want to say
But don't know how to say
them

I am lost in thought
Just thinking about you

How I wish I could show my
devotion
But it would never compare to
the emotion I feel for you

These feelings deep inside
Are hard to bring to the surface

My heart says go
But my head says no

I am not sure which to follow
I just wish you could give me a
sign to yes or no

Dream to Reality

The last time I saw your pretty
face
You stopped me and stole my
breath away
I took one look at you
And it was plain to see
You were my destiny

I'll sacrifice for you
And dedicate my life to you
If only for a night I could hold
you in my arms
And with just one whisper tell
you how I feel
I'd surrender everything just to
be with you

I'm here without you
But you're still on my lonely
mind
And anywhere I go
I try but can't seem to get
myself
To think of anything but you

Under the power of the bright
stars
I confess to you
I can't live if living is without
you
You are here with me in my
dreams
But it's plain to see dreams can
become reality

Simply Irresistible

These feelings inside
Run so deep
They just make me feel lost
In an irresistible trance

I don't know which way is up,
Which way is down
I don't even know what's going
on around me
All I know is this feeling is
incredible

It's like nothing I have ever felt
before
It feels weird
Yet totally amazing
It's an unspoken comfort

Only two words come to mind
To describe this deep
And warm feeling
Simply Irresistible

Lakeside Beauty

Sitting by the lake
Watching the stars
Light up the sky

Visions dancing around in my
head
Then the stars form
As I see your pretty face
Forming together by the night
sky

I reach out to brush
My hand across your cheek
But you're to far away to reach

I see your smile
Then you wink at me
And I smile back

Only knowing that…
No matter how far away
We will always have each other

Everlasting Pain

The sharp jagged edge
And hallow point reaches the
crack
Slowly making its way through
Making the crack bigger

The liquid slowly coming out
As the pain grows bigger
Sharp and hard to fight
Its slowly breaking as the pain
grows worse

You say you hope all will be ok
That you are sorry and don't
want it
You say the words I want to
hear
But not in the way they were
meant to be said

How can you sit there and ask
If I will be ok
When you know the response
Before you even ask the

question

Of course I'm not ok
I am in pain
Worse then you can ever
imagine
I tell you this now my heart
will never be the same again

Way down in the water
Across the lake
I saw her face
Her smile so bright

Her eyes glistened to the color
of the water
Her voice so soft
I could hardly tell what she was
saying
But I was hooked

From the first dive
To the last stroke
I knew I had to meet her
To know she was all I wanted

She looked my way
She winked at me
Then swan away

Sitting Here Thinking

I've been sitting here
Trying to find myself
But what would happen if they
ever knew
I can't live forever

It's so easy to be lost
And I've been gone; I've been
gone for way to long
It seems no matter what I do
I just stare out my window

Dreaming of what could be
And if I'd end up happy
It just tears my heart in two

All the days collide
One less perfect than the next
I've got bruises on my heart
and sometimes I get dark
Love just isn't much of a friend
of mine

It's hard to hang out in crowds

I just want someone who will
help me
Out of the darkness and into the
sun
But my heart keeps callin and I
keep on fallen

You will never get to see these
tears I cry
Because you're the one who
looks right through me
That is why...
I've been sitting here
Trying to find myself

Guided Dream

How can I make you see
That I'm torn apart inside
Feeling all alone with no
support

I just want to hold you in my
arms
Look into your eyes
And know you are the one

I wanna cuddle by the fire
And with one whisper tell you
everything
Tell you how…

You are my fire,
You are my passion,
Most of all you are my
everything

This I wish I could say
As I lie here
Feeling cold and lonely

Wondering will I ever…
Find where you are,
Will I ever know
If I can get to you

Please guide me
And tell me how to find her
And how to get to her

Ashley Massaro

Born on the shores of Long
Island, NY
Was a blue-green eyed tomboy
Who soon would turn model

From beauty pageants to
modeling
To 2005 Diva Search winner
This 5'5" beauty would soon
shock the world

With a bachelors of science in
communications
This Bangin' star would soon
show herself off
As a cover girl for many
magazines

From Raw to Smackdown
This diva gives it her all in and
out of the ring
All the way to the Tribal
Council of Survivor

Whether you like her or hate
her
Once you see this Dirty Diva in
action
You will truly be star-struck

Dream Girl

My heart yearns for you
With a love so rare and true
I think about you all the time
Dreaming of holding you in my
arms one day soon

Wishing and hoping for this
miracle
I would do anything for this to
be true
A dream to reality is all I wish
for

I would give anything for this
chance
Whether it be selling my soul to
Satan
Or ending my life

It would totally be worth it
Just to be with you
For just one night of total and
endless bliss

I wish to say this to you one
day
Only hoping this message
Will come true one day soon

Because my heart yearns for
you
With a love so rare and true
I think about you all the time
Just dreaming on holding you
in my arms one day soon

Changing Places

Sitting here in Vegas
Roaming the streets again
Looking for the familiar
Only to see the unknown

Things are changing
And at a fast pace
Change is good
But confusing at times

People are changing
People are disappearing
Some even lost contact
With who they are

Places are changing too
Everything is looking different
Change is always good for
places
But too much change can hurt

I love changes
On occasions
But not all the time

This is my changing places
story

Confusion

My head is spinning in a vortex
of confusion
Not knowing which was is up
or down
My heart says no,
But my head says let's go
I'm moving in the right
direction
Though I'm going nowhere fast

All is lost but yet still there
I'm burning up inside while my
body is on the verge of freezing
My soul is fluttering with
agitation
While my brain commands to
stay calm
I wish I could say it feels
normal to be lost
But then I would just be lying

I just wish I could make you
see

That doubts in life…
Are all apart of being alive.

Drive of My Life

My head is stuck in overdrive
My mind is lot in thought
My heart doesn't know which
to follow
I can't figure out which way is
up or down
Left feels like right
Right feels like wrong
I don't know what to do
anymore
I feel I've hit a block wall
In which I don't have the
strength to break through
There is no reverse or 4 wheel
drive
I'm stuck in neutral
I'm giving up on everything
And going for the obvious road
The road in which everyone
else follows
The road called life

My Dying Wish

I tell you this
My world is complicated
So consider this...
I am me and
There is never a day that goes
by
That I don't get stronger
It may amaze you to know
How I deal with all the pain
inside my head

You always seem to come
back for me
With these new stories of why
you left
They might have worked in
another life
But they only bring me to life
here

Every time you seem to catch
me when I fall
Don't bother because my eyes
are wide open

I know you will stand in my
way,
But please remember this
isn't my first taste of love

Because of you I have pieces
of me still undiscovered
I am running on this lonely
road of faith
And I'm here without you
although you are always on
my mind
Seems like everything I do is
for you and not me

All that I live for now is for
you to love me for me
It is my last resort
That with every last breathe
I'll find you and show you...

That love can show you
everything
So close your eyes and listen
to your heart
Don't tell me what it says,

Just take me away
Because I am bleeding love
for you
And with just one whisper I'll
tell you how…
I knew I loved you before I
met you,
How you are my immortal,
And how you are my happy
ending
Until the day I slip away

I hope when I am gone
That you will lock me up in
your heart shaped box
I will always remember
where you are when I am
gone
So baby don't throw it all
away
Because you are the one I
want
So please can I go now?

The Missing Link (Dream Girl)

I spend night and day thinking
of you
I see you in my dreams yet
your face is a blur
I wonder who you are
Your voice so sweet
Your hair so soft and smooth

I hold you in my arms every
night
Just praying that one day I will
see who you are
Your kisses so soft and
sensuous

I will search the ends of the
earth for you
As my soul aches deep down
inside
To know who you are

I have never known anyone
Who can make me feel this way

But I know that when I find
you
You will let me know who you
are

Haunting Past

You are gone
Yet you are still here
Your remains 6 feet under
But your spirit remains next to
me

The loss was tragic
But the feelings still the same
I enjoy your company
And comfort so long as you
stay

The light has yet to find you
That I am thankful for
For without you by my side
I would be lost forever

You are with me now
Soon I will be with you forever
Life is short
But eternity is forever

I know you will be there
When I leave this place to join

you
Together hand in hand
We can go through together

Screaming Torture

I see you standing there in the
darkness of light
You try to speak but all that is
heard is an ear-piercing shriek
The more you try to speak the
worse it gets
The pain you speak is
deafening and my ears are
bleeding

I am yearning to understand
what you are trying to say
Your signals of language are so
confusing I can't make out your
words
I try to read your eyes but they
are dark as night with no way
in
I am on my knees begging you
to let me in and help you

Don't be afraid to let it show
For I will take what scares you
most and hold it deep inside

Let me in and we will battle
your fears together
Reach out to me and I will
show you the light that life can
give you

I know that you're wounded
You know that I'm here to save
you
Take my hand I will mend all
your wounds and heal your
scars
I w show you a world filled
with understanding
So please…

Don't be afraid to let it show
For I will take what scares you
most and hold it deep inside
Let me in and we will battle
your fears together
Reach out to me and I will
show you the light that life can
give you

Finding The Inner Me

I've been sitting here
Trying to find myself
But what would happen if they
ever knew
I can't live forever

It's so easy to be lost
And I've been gone, I've been
gone for way too long
It seems no matter what I do
I just stare out my window

Dreaming of what could be
And if I'd end up happy
It just tears my heart in two

All the days collide
One less perfect than the next
I've got bruises on my heart
and sometimes I get dark
Love just isn't much of a friend
of mine

It's hard to hang out in crowds

I just want someone who will
help me
Out of the darkness and into the
sun
But my heart keeps callin and I
keep on fallen

You will never get to see these
tears I cry
Because you're the one who
looks right through me
That is why…
I've been sitting here
Trying to find myself

HELP!!

When you are around
My hears breaks knowing I
can't be with you
Yet still I am happy when you
are here

Just knowing that you give me
friendship
Is all I need to stay happy
But these feelings are driving
me crazy

It's comforting yet confusing
My head says run,
My heart says stay

Not knowing which road to
follow
Has left me in a painful mess
The end result both different
yet happy

With no one but you to turn to
I don't know what to say

Or where to start

Your guidance I seek
Yet not wanting to tell you the
situation
To save myself from
embarrassment

Destiny of Love

The last time I saw your pretty
face
You stopped me and stole my
breath away
I took one look at you
And it was plain to see
You were my destiny

I'll sacrifice for you
And dedicate my life to you
If only for a night I could hold
you in my arms
And with just one whisper tell
you how I feel
I'd surrender everything just to
be with you

I'm here without you
But you're still on my lonely
mind
And anywhere I go
I try but can't seem to get
myself
To think of anything but you

Under the power of the bright
stars
I confess to you
I can't live if living is without
you
You are here with me in my
dreams
But its plain to see dreams can
become reality

You Are My Everything

How can I make you see…
That I'm torn apart inside
Feeling all alone with no
support

I just want to hold you in my
arms
Look into your eyes
And know you are the one

I wanna cuddle by the fire
And with one whisper tell you
everything
Tell you how…

You are my fire,
You are my passion,
Most of all you are my
everything

This I wish I could say
As I lyre here
Feeling cold and lonely

Wondering will I ever…
Find where you are,
will I ever know
If I can get to you

Please guide me
And tell me how to find her
And how to get to her

Words

These words I want to say
But don't know how to say
them

I am lost in thought
Just thinking about you

How I wish I could show my
devotion
But it could never compare to
the emotion I feel for you

These feelings deep inside
Are hard to bring to the surface

My heart says go
But my head says no

I am not sure which to follow
I just wish you could give me a
sign to yes or no

Delicate Tears

Why do you cry
With tears so light and gentle
I feel them caress my cheek
As I hold you close

I don't know what to do
But to just sit and hold you
Hold you until you are ready
Ready to tell me why you are
crying

It bothers me to know
That something has hurt you
So deep inside
That you can't bring it up to tell
me

Whatever it is
I am here to listen
Whenever you are ready to talk
Just say the words and I will
understand

I just want to understand you

And wish I could feel the pain
that you do
Just look inside to open up
And when you do, you will
realize I am here

No One Has To Know

No one has to know who you
are
No… no one has to know
where you are
No one, no one, no one
No one has to know…

What you did
No… no one has to know how
you did it all
No one, no one, no one
No one has to know…

Why you did it all for love
No… no one has to know
No one, no one, no one
No one has to know…

Why I'm tangled up
Tangled up in you…
No… no one has to know
No one, no one, no one

No one has to know who you

are
No… no one has to know
where you are
No one, no one, no one
No one has to know

Smiling Depression

I don't smile because I am
unhappy
I don't know when or if I will
smile again
Life has been rough
And I have gone through a lot

Enough to bring me into a state,
A horrible state that is hard to
escape
A deep dark state of depression
Hard to battle and get through

It is tough to battle and
overcome
Many have tried and few have
succeeded
I just go through life3 with a
fake smile
Which leads people to believe I
am ok

Though deep down I am
hurting,

To an extent I don't talk about
my problems
I try to keep them to myself
So no one knows but me

I am a very private person
Who doesn't like to talk
I am a listener no a talker
That is why I suffer from
smiling depression

Magic Moment

I listen…
But don't hear
I only understand

I understand
The passion and emotion
That seeps through your words

I feel I've known you forever
You were just a poster on my
wall
Now I see you all the time

You were a dream in my head
Now you are a reality in my life

You are my heaven
And you have my heart

I could sleep all the time
But feel I would be wasting
away without you

With every word you speak

You mean more and more to
me

You are living proof
That dreams come true

You are the locket in my life
You hold something very
amazing
A special treasure never
forgotten

You hold the key and
combination
To something so dear to me
In which I refer to as my heart

Invisible To You

You say you see me all the time
But you don't even know my
name
I feel invisible to you

I don't even think
You know when I'm around
Cause I feel invisible to you

Do you even know me?
Do you recognize me?
Do you even see me?

I think you see right past me
While I see right into your eyes
And feel invisible to you

You walk on by me
You don't even know I'm alive
I feel invisible to you

Two Worlds

In this world of bright lights
and stars
My dreams can be seen clearly
I am oblivious to all naysayers
I can do anything and go
anywhere .

In the real world of darkness
and heart ache
Nothing can be accomplished
without love and support
The naysayers rule life and
freedom
They say who makes it and
who doesn't

Two worlds lived
Two worlds of opposites
Two worlds that will never
collide
Two worlds where opposites
definitely don't attract

My life is set in these two

worlds
One in which I love and enjoy
One in which I feel captive and
can't escape
Only wishing I had the power
to collide Two Worlds

These are my two worlds lived
Two worlds of opposites
My two worlds that will never
collide
The two worlds where
opposites definitely don't
attract

Hardships

Everyone has hardships
Whether your rich, poor, or in
the middle
We are all the same
Some just don't realize it
Some don't have anything and
struggle
Some have very little and
struggle
Some have a lot and yet still
struggle
And then there are those that
have everything
Yet you don't see it but they to
struggle

These are some ways we all
have hardships
Some have nothing yet struggle
to get something
Some have something yet
struggle to gain but not lose
what they have
While those with everything

struggle to keep
What they have and not lose it
all

So whether you have it all or
nothing
Remember everyone has
hardships and everyone
struggles
Always remind yourself that we
are all the same
In every equal way

Life of Hell

There was a time when I was
all alone
I wake up in the morning
And I've never felt like this
before

Feels like I'm living in a slow
hell
It's getting dark, to dark to see
That long black cloud is
coming down

And I wonder...
Why do you always do this to
me
I feel your blood turning cold

Can you feel it in your soul
That my heart is broken
And the pain wont go away

I just need to know if I can
breath
Cause in this head my thoughts

are deep
Trying to figure out this life

I was left to cry there
Grinning with a lost stare
Wishing someone would cure
this pain

I'm giving up on everything
And what more can I say
But so much for my happy
ending

Invisible To The Mind

I feel invisible to you
But are you aware of how you
make me feel
I'm longing for the love and the
logical

I've gotta make a change
And take a risk
But I don't know what to say

I'm lost in my thoughts
And it kills me now just to see
you
I try my hardest to forget
everything

Just so I can say those special
words
But I fear rejection
And the demons that come with
it

I'm torn into pieces
And broken up deep inside

Just wishing you can mend the
pieces together

I just need to know
If in your soul
You feel the same way about
me
As I do for you

Yearning Love

My heart yearns for you
With a love so rare and true
I think about you all the time
Dreaming of holding you in my
arms one day soon

Wishing and hoping for this
miracle
I would do anything for this to
be true
A dream to reality is all I wish
for

I would give anything for this
chance
Whether it be selling my soul to
Satan
Or ending my life

It would totally be worth it
Just to be with you
For just one night of total and
endless bliss

I wish to say this to you one
day
Only hoping this message
Will come true one day soon

Because my heart yearns for
you
With a love so rare and true
I think about you all the time
Just dreaming of holding you in
my arms one day soon

A Fools Dream Crushed

I had the chance of a lifetime
And it might have been my last
I said no the first time
Now I am in regret

The time has come
Here and now
To tell the world
How I feel

I let you go far away
It was too far to be
Now you are back
But still to far for me

I was lost without you
Day in and day out
I try to find my way
Back to your heart I look

We spend time alone
It feels like a lifetime
Passing by as we sit under the
tree

Just you and me

We sit and talk
About different things
Then we hit sad roads
You move into my arms
Which I use to hold you

Now feeling like an eternity
I have never had these emotions
before
The feeling of comfort and joy

It feels like I have found
The missing piece to the puzzle
Which will make me happy
again
That piece is you

But it's not all there just yet
Part of it is missing
Just like part of my heart is
missing
It is all tied together
Waiting for you to untie it and
Make it whole again

I think about you
During the day
And wish I could
See you at night

This I say to you
Not because I love you
But because my heart
Needs to be completed

I have put all the pieces
Back together though it took a
while
But realized one was missing
And that is the one that is in
Your possession and wont be
Complete without you to go
with it

So I want you to hold on to it
Until you think it is time
To make the puzzle complete
Or to make it incomplete
forever
By destroying the soul piece

This I say to you
With love from my heart
And plenty of passion
For the one and only love I
have for you

Made in the USA
Charleston, SC
18 September 2012